SPOT THE DIFFERENCE

A group study course for Lent

NICK FAWCETT

**kevin
mayhew**

First published in 2006 by

KEVIN MAYHEW LTD
Buxhall, Stowmarket, Suffolk, IP14 3BW
E-mail: info@kevinmayhew.com
www.kevinmayhew.com

9 8 7 6 5 4 3 2 1

ISBN 1 84417 707 6
Catalogue No. 1500964

Cover design by Sara-Jane Came
Edited and typeset by Katherine Laidler

Printed and bound in Great Britain

Contents

Introduction

'You're a Christian, are you?' said the stranger. 'So what?' I'd thought he was interested up till then, eager to find out more, and up to a point perhaps he was, but his comment oozed scepticism, and as we talked further I realised he had good reason. He'd known many Christians over the years, in fact been part of a church himself for a while, but he'd grown disillusioned, the glib talk he'd heard during that time about love, joy and goodness failing to find a corresponding echo in people's lives. Christians, he argued, have no monopoly on such things, many non-believers indeed putting them to shame. And, of course, he was right. We show the same faults and weaknesses as anyone else, there being precious little about our lives to distinguish them from those around us. God forbid that anyone might judge Christ by the yardstick of our discipleship, but that, unfortunately, is precisely what many *will* do. Of course, we can argue in mitigation that the Church is as much for sinners as saints, but that doesn't mean our flawed discipleship doesn't matter. Our daily aim should be to grow more like Jesus, striving with God's help to serve him better.

Traditionally, Lent is a time of examination directed towards that end; a time for recognising where our commitment is lacking and seeking to deepen our faith. The challenge is succinctly put in those stark words of my interrogator: 'So what?' What difference does being a Christian make to your life and what difference *should* it make? Are you simply going through the motions or does your discipleship actually show? In this book we consider five ways in which commitment should manifest itself: in a quality of love, a spontaneity of witness, a disposition of joy, a generosity of spirit and a vibrant inner faith. Of course there are other aspects we could focus on – peace, truth and hope, for example – but if these five alone were truly to characterise our life, what an impact we would make. Focus upon such things, seeking with God's help to make them more fully a part of who and what you are, and, make no mistake, people will spot the difference!

NICK FAWCETT

Session 1
A love that shows

Theme

The 'new commandment' of Jesus was that we should love one another, but how far does love actually distinguish our lives as Christians?

Opening prayer

O God of love, we ask you to give us love:
    love in our thinking,
    love in our speaking,
    love in our doing,
    and love in the hidden places of our souls;
    love of those with whom we find it hard to bear,
    and love of those who find it hard to bear with us;
    love of those with whom we work,
    and love of those with whom we take our ease;
    so that at length we may be worthy to dwell with you,
    who are eternal love.
Amen.

William Temple (1881–1944)

Setting the scene

Let love be the controlling force in your life, just as Christ loved us, giving himself up as a fragrant offering and sacrifice pleasing to God. (Ephesians 5:2)

The commandments 'You shall not commit adultery, shall not murder; shall not steal, shall not yearn for what belongs to someone else' – these and indeed all others – are encapsulated in a single command: 'Love your neighbour as yourself. If you love others, it stands to reason you will not wrong them; to love, in other words, is to obey the Law.' (Romans 13:9, 10)

Activity

Take a look at the pictures on the opposite page. Can you spot eleven differences between them? (The answers can be found in the Appendix.)

Talk together afterwards about what sort of differences there should be in the life of a Christian, and how far these ought to show.

Introduction

It's never easy to summarise something important in a few words, but with Christianity we're invited to do just that, and by none other than Jesus himself. For him all the commandments and everything God requires of us boil down to one thing: love. So, unsurprisingly, the New Testament writers have much to say on this theme, time and again emphasising the importance of love in any authentic discipleship; this, more than any other, is the central message of the gospel and the defining mark of God's people. Quite simply, as John reminds us, if we do not love then we do not know God – the two belong together. But do we love in a way that is any different to those around us? If asked to describe how your faith comes across to them, would anyone you know include love in their answer? The following passages bring home just how important a question that is.

Exploring the Scriptures

John 13:34, 35; 15:12

I give you now a new commandment: that you love one another. You must love each other just as I have loved you. If you have such love, people everywhere will recognise you as my disciples. This, then, is my commandment – that you love one another as I have loved you.

1 John 2:9, 10; 4:7-12, 20, 21

If we claim to be in the light but hate others, we are, in fact, even now in the darkness, but if we love others, then we live in the light, and nothing in us will lead others to sin. Dear friends, let us love one another, because love comes from God; all those who love are born of God and know God. Whoever does not love knows nothing of God, for God is love. God demonstrated his love like this – he sent his only Son into the world in order that we might live through him. In this is love, not that we loved God but that he loved us and sent his Son to be the expiation for our sins. Dear friends, given that God has loved us like this, shouldn't we love one another similarly in turn? Although no one has actually ever seen God, if we love one another, then he is one with us and his love is perfected in us. We cannot love him, whom we have never seen, unless we love others, whom we have seen. Christ's command to us is this: those who love God must also love others.

Prayer

Lord Jesus Christ,
    fill us, we pray, with your light
    that we may reflect your wondrous glory.
So fill us with your love
    that we may count nothing too small to do for you,

nothing too much to give,
and nothing too hard to bear.
Amen.

St Ignatius Loyola (1491–1556)

Enlarging the picture

To some, the Christian's talk of love is just wishy-washy idealism, a way of glossing over the need for moral decision-making, avoiding taking a stand on controversial issues. Loving one another, they say, is all very well, but what does it involve in practice? We need guidelines, rules, boundaries – clearly marked lines that spell out how love ought to show itself in specific situations.

Is that right? I can understand the concern, for love undeniably leads different people to act in different ways, what seems right to one seeming wrong to another. But is that not precisely the point of Jesus' teaching? There are no one-size-fits-all regulations, love indeed having to decide afresh in each and every circumstance. It may seem woolly, but in fact it's the most demanding way of all, for it must meet people where they are rather than take refuge in moral certainties.

To illustrate what that means, I want to paint for you four simple scenarios, each leading into points for discussion concerning issues that are anything but simple.

Scenario 1

Jack walked cheerfully through the school gates, then froze in dismay as he spotted a group of youths loitering ahead. He'd come to know them all too well across the years, their repeated bullying having made his life a misery and cast a shadow over what should have been carefree times. Hurriedly he pressed himself against the wall and tried to sidle back the way he'd come, hoping he hadn't been noticed, but it was no good – the gang were advancing menacingly towards him, grinning as they approached.

Should he run? He wanted to, but what was the point? They'd catch him soon enough and punish him all the more for their exertions. So he just stood there, waiting for the fist in the stomach, the kick on the shin, the slap across the face, determined if nothing else to keep the tears from his eyes during his ritual humiliation.

They were upon him now, yet no fist came – no sickening thud and writhing on the floor in agony . . . nothing! Dimly he was aware of the ringleader speaking, and suddenly it dawned on Jack that the words were not of insult but apology and the outstretched hand a gesture of friendship rather than aggression. The most feared boy in the school – his name for so long a byword for brutality and aggression – was speaking of faith, remorse, and new beginnings; he who had shown no mercy now seeking forgiveness. Could it be true? Surely not! But Jack wasn't going to argue the toss. Hesitantly he shook the proffered hand, still expecting some sting in the tail, and when none came he raced off – baffled, bewildered, but, above all, relieved.

Discussion points

- Does that story seem a little far-fetched? You might think so, but you'd be wrong, for *I* was the one being bullied and the ringleader in question was literally transformed overnight, going on to become a full-time Christian evangelist! Can you think of other people who have changed as dramatically from an attitude of hate to love? Have you personally known anyone transformed in this way? Are there people you've given up on or do you still believe they can change?

- Few of us will experience such a radical transformation from hate to love, simply because we didn't actually hate in the first place, but is love more a part of your life now than it was before you became a Christian? Jesus spoke of loving one's enemy. Could you have done that in Jack's shoes?

- Jesus speaks of people knowing we're his disciples by our love. Is that realistic? Do you think people see a distinctive quality of love in your life? Do you think they see *any* love in your life?

Scenario 2

Private Taylor dived down into the crater as a shell exploded nearby, accompanied by yet another burst of machinegun fire. He couldn't take much more of this – hour upon hour grovelling in the mud waiting for the bullet or shard of shrapnel that would put an end to his war, maybe even his life, as it had done for so many of his colleagues. He'd seen hundreds cut down beside him, their bodies mangled beyond recognition, and the sights and sounds of battle, too dreadful for words, haunted his thoughts day and night. How he hated this place, and, most of all, how he hated the enemy who made it necessary for him to be there. If he could only get his hands on them, he'd make them pay.

A sudden moaning broke into his thoughts – animal-like, stomach-churning – the sound of someone in agony, piteously appealing for help. He turned reluctantly, fearful of what he might see . . . then gasped, in relief and shock. It wasn't one of his comrades, but a German, his face a welter of blood, an arm almost severed, and a tangle of shattered bones protruding from a gaping wound in his chest.

Suddenly all hatred was gone, replaced simply by compassion for a fellow human being in need. He took his hip flask of rum and put it to the lips of the stricken soldier, who drank urgently, desperate to numb the pain. Blinking back tears from his eyes, Taylor gently cradled the man's head in his arms, cursing now not the enemy but this foul and futile war. There was nothing he could do, nothing *anyone* could do, except offer what support he could as the life ebbed slowly away. The wounded man shuddered in a last paroxysm of pain, then looked up with a smile of gratitude before his eyes glazed over and looked out no more.

Discussion points

- What things stop you from loving others? Are there situations in which you fail to love as much as you should? Are you willing to enlarge on these?

- What does love in the Christian sense actually mean? What *doesn't* it mean? Does anything set apart the love Christians show to that shown by others? Do you think it should?

- Can love conquer hate or is this simply naïve idealism? Would you see the non-violent campaigns of Martin Luther King or Mahatma Gandhi, or the resistance of those like Desmond Tutu, Allan Boesak and Trevor Huddleston to apartheid in South Africa, as examples of love in action? If so, what do you make of the fact that Gandhi was a Hindu? Consider also the subsequent work of the Truth and Reconciliation Commission. What impact has this had and what might have happened without it?

Scenario 3

'It's not fair!' snarled Jason, glaring furiously at his mother.

'It's perfectly fair, dear,' she answered, 'as you well know.'

'It's not,' snapped Jason. 'Why can't I borrow the money if I want to? Gareth's dad allowed *him* to borrow even more.'

'Maybe he did, but that's not the point. For one thing, you can't afford to repay it and you certainly don't want a mountain of debt hanging round your neck. For another, I honestly think you'll be wasting your money and be far better spending it on something else. And anyway, you don't *deserve* it at the moment – not after that scrape you got yourself into, for which, may I remind you, your father and I are still having to pay.'

Jason, however, was having none of it. 'If you really loved me,' he muttered, 'you'd *give* me as much as I need. You just don't care, do you?'

'I *do* care,' sighed his mother, well used to his emotional blackmail, 'and that's precisely why the answer's still no. Giving in would be the easy option, but eventually it would do none of us any good. I'm not enjoying this, Jason, despite what you think, but it's because I love you so much that I won't change my mind. Hopefully you'll understand one day.'

But Jason wasn't ready to listen any longer. With a snort he got up and stormed out the room, slamming the door behind him.

Discussion points

- Are there times when love involves being cruel to be kind? Can you give examples? Have you experienced this firsthand?

- Do you see love as an easy or hard option? Can it be used as a way of sitting on the fence and avoiding complex moral issues or is the opposite true?

- Have there been times when love has led you to question biblical teaching or established church doctrine?

Scenario 4

The true story of Nicky Cruz will be familiar to many from the powerful 1970 film *The Cross and the Switchblade*. Brought up in Puerto Rico by parents steeped in witchcraft, Nicky was soon no stranger to trouble and when, in 1955, aged 16, he and his brother were sent to live in New York City, he quickly became part of the infamous Mau Maus gang, equally swiftly rising to become their leader. Street-fights, drug-taking, robbery and murder became a way of life for him until David Wilkerson, an itinerate preacher, began crusading in the ghetto, persevering with his mission despite Nicky beating him up and threatening to kill him if he continued. When Wilkerson hired a hall in the area for an evangelistic rally, Cruz decided to make good his threat, but when he arrived at the scene and heard Wilkerson preaching, something came over him, and instead of attacking the preacher he knelt down and prayed, asking forgiveness from both Wilkerson and God. He went on to

15

train for the ministry, returning to the ghettoes to win for Christ many of his old gang, including their new leader. The founder of Nicky Cruz Outreach, devoted to helping troubled young people, and of 'halfway houses' aimed at the rehabilitation of drug addicts, Cruz has preached the gospel across the world.

Discussion points

- Can you think of other people who have been shining examples of love? What was it that motivated them?

- Are Christians meant to love everyone? Is this possible in the real world? Is there a danger of sentimentalising, offering pious platitudes? Could you, for example, feel love for a terrorist, murderer or rapist?

- Has the Church/religion been an agency for love or hatred across the years? Does this raise issues that Christianity and we as Christians need to face?

Food for thought

Consider the following proverbs and quotations. What are they saying? Which do you find most helpful? What are their strengths and weaknesses? Do you agree or disagree with the point they're making?

- Love cures people – both the ones who give it and the ones who receive it. (Carl Menninger)

- Give me such love for God and men, as will blot out all hatred and bitterness. (Dietrich Bonhoeffer)

- I have decided to stick with love. Hate is too great a burden to bear. (Martin Luther King)

- People are lonely because they build walls instead of bridges. (J. F. Newton)

- If I love the world as it is, I am already changing it. A first fragment of the world has been changed, and that is my own heart. (Petru Dumitriu)

- Love is the movement, effusion and advancement of the heart toward the good. (St Francis de Sales)

- Have a heart that never hardens, and a temper that never tires, and a touch that never hurts. (Charles Dickens)

- Only love can bring individual beings to their perfect completion as individuals because only love takes possession of them and unites them by what lies deepest within them. (Teilhard de Chardin)

- Where there is no love, pour love in, and you will draw out love. (St John of the Cross)

- To love is to wish the other's highest good. (R. H. Benson)

- I beg you to stamp everything with the seal of love, nothing else will last. (Elizabeth of the Trinity)

- We have just enough religion to make us hate, but not enough to make us love one another. (Jonathan Swift)

- Love seeks one thing only: the good of the one loved. It leaves all the other secondary effects to take care of themselves. Love, therefore, is its own reward. (Thomas Merton)

- Love is all we have, the only way that each can help the other. (Euripides)

- Some day, after mastering the winds, the waves, the tides, and gravity, we shall harness for God the energies of love, and then, for the second time in the history of the world, man will have discovered fire. (Teilhard de Chardin)

Prayer

You make it sound so simple, Lord,
    summarising the Law and the Prophets,
    the way to life itself,
    in one simple command:
    to love.
But we don't find it simple at all.
We find it harder than we ever imagined,
    both understanding what love involves,
    and then acting upon it.

When we are faced with complex situations,
    and are unsure what love asks of us,
    afraid we may hurt instead of heal,
    harm instead of help,
    teach us your way,
    the way of love incarnate.

When love is demanding,
    calling for sacrifices we would rather not make,
    choices we would prefer to ignore,
    commitment we are reluctant to give,
    a response that goes against the grain,
    teach us your way,
    the way of love incarnate.

When we find others hard to love,
    our attitude towards them clouded by hurt, jealousy,
    pride and anger,
    so much that poisons relationships,
    teach us your way,
    the way of love incarnate.

When we are indifferent to others,
    so wrapped up in our own world,

our own concerns and interests,
that we overlook their needs,
teach us your way,
the way of love incarnate.

When our words say one thing but our lives say another,
our talk of a special kind of love
belied by the mediocrity of our discipleship,
the lack of anything even remotely distinctive,
teach us your way,
the way of love incarnate.
Amen.

Completing the picture

Below are some biblical verses exploring God's call to love.
Reflect on them quietly together and then discuss any further
thoughts arising from them.

- If I speak in the tongues of people or angels, but do not have
love, I become nothing more than a blasting trumpet or clashing
cymbal. If I have the gift of prophecy and understand all
mysteries and all knowledge, and if I have faith such as to
remove mountains, yet do not have love, then I am nothing. If I
dispense all my goods and surrender my body to be burned,
yet do not have love, it profits me nothing. Love is patient and
kind; it is not jealous or puffed up with its own importance,
vaunting itself before others, nor does it knowingly cause offence.
It does not seek its own well-being, is not easily provoked, and
does not think evil or rejoice in wrongdoing but rejoices rather
in the truth. It embraces all things, believes all things, hopes
all things, endures all things. Love is eternal. Three things
continue – faith, hope and love – and the greatest of them is love.
(1 Corinthians 13:1-8a, 13)

- You have become a new person, your minds being renewed into the likeness of the one who created you. So then, as God's chosen ones, holy and greatly loved, clothe yourselves with compassion, kindness, humility, meekness and patience, being merciful to one another and forgiving any quarrel you may have; in other words, forgive as the Lord forgave you. Above all, clothe yourselves with love, which binds everything together in perfect harmony. (Colossians 3:9b, 10, 12-14)

- My advice to you is to love your enemies, do good to those who hate you, and pray for whoever mistreats you. Do for others precisely what you'd like them to do to you. Why should you expect a blessing for loving only those who love you? Even sinners do that. (Luke 6:27, 28, 31, 32)

Blessing

Gracious God,
    may your love fill us,
    transform us,
    sustain us
    and flow through us,
    this day and always.
Amen.

Session 2
An allegiance that shows

Theme

Jesus calls us to be his witnesses, making known the gospel to all, but how far and in what ways do our lives testify to him?

Opening prayer

Lord,
   make me a messenger of your love.
To the searching heart
   send me with your word;
   to the aching heart
   send me with your peace;
   to the broken heart
   send me with your love.
However small or wide my world, Lord,
   let me warm it with the promise that you care.
Amen.
Author unknown

Setting the scene

Do not be embarrassed about witnessing for our Lord, or about me being a prisoner for Christ's sake. I urge you, rather, to share with me in suffering for the good news, trusting in God's power to see you through. (2 Timothy 1:8)

Scripture tells us, 'Everyone who calls on the name of the Lord will be saved.' How, though, can they call on one in whom they have not believed, and believe in one of whom they have never heard? How can they hear without someone to proclaim him, and how can anyone proclaim unless they are sent? As Scripture also says, 'How wonderful is the arrival of messengers bringing good news!' (Romans 10:13-15)

Activity

Take a look at the chart below and see if you can spot the odd one out in each case.

A	Ounce	2
E	Gramme	4
T	Pound	7
U	Stone	8

Rose	Lion	March
Snowdrop	Cow	July
Daffodil	Sheep	May
Crocus	Horse	June

London	Liverpool	Silk
Bristol	Manchester Utd	Cotton
York	Tottenham Hotspur	Nylon
Cheltenham	Southend Utd	Wool

Hebrews	Holland	Rain
Exodus	France	Snow
Romans	Belgium	Frost
Acts	Brazil	Ice

Level	Football	Nahum
Wide	Golf	Nehemiah
Deed	Rugby	Ruth
Tenet	Hockey	Timothy

Chat together about the difficulties of standing out in a crowd and sticking up for one's faith.

Introduction

Sharing our faith isn't easy, is it? Most of us, for one thing, are hampered by an innate reserve, an unwillingness to push our beliefs upon others, however important we may deem them to be. Many also find it hard to find the right words, struggling to express themselves with anywhere near the clarity they would like. But those are only part of the problem. What compounds them is the prevailing attitude today towards Christianity and the difficulty of finding any way of speaking about events of two thousands years ago, and what they mean to us, in terms that sound natural, fresh and, above all, relevant. Even as I was writing these lines, I had a knock on the door and was met on opening it by a member of a local fellowship handing out promotional material. It was well intentioned, and I applauded both his courage and the motivation behind the initiative, but I couldn't help wondering what most would make of it – whether the approach would come across as one of genuine interest in them as people or as yet another attempt to peddle religion and gain new recruits for a dying cause. Most of us, I suspect, genuinely wish we could share our faith, but feel the odds are stacked against us, so we subconsciously thrust the issue aside, hoping it will go away. That's an understandable temptation, but, as the following passages remind us, it's one we cannot afford to succumb to.

Exploring the Scriptures

Matthew 28:18-20

Jesus approached and said to them, 'All power in heaven and earth has been given to me. So go and make disciples of all people, baptising them in the name of the Father, the Son and the Holy Spirit, teaching them to obey whatever I have commanded you. I guarantee to be with you, to the very end of time.

Acts 4:1-3, 5-10, 12, 13, 18-20

While Peter and John were addressing the people, the priests, together with the captain of the temple and the Sadducees, approached them, incensed at their teaching the people and preaching of the resurrection of the dead through Jesus. In consequence, they arrested them, placing them, since night was falling, in custody until the next day. On the next day, their leaders, elders and scribes gathered in Jerusalem, together with the high priest Annas, and other members of the high-priestly family – Caiaphas, John and Alexander. The prisoners having been brought in before them, they began the interrogation. 'On whose authority or in whose name did you do this?' they demanded. Filled with the Holy Spirit, Peter answered, 'Leaders of the people and elders, assuming you're questioning us today because you're anxious to know how we helped heal someone who was formerly sick, then I want you and all Israel to understand that this man stands fit and well before you now through the authority of Jesus Christ of

Nazareth – the man whom you crucified but who God raised from the dead. Salvation comes through no one else but him, there being no other name under heaven by which people can be saved.

On seeing the boldness of Peter and John, uneducated and ordinary men, their accusers were amazed, recognising them as companions of Jesus. They called them and ordered them not to speak or teach at all in the name of Jesus. But Peter and John answered them, 'Whether it is right in God's eyes to listen to you rather than to God, you must judge; for we cannot help speaking of everything we have seen and heard.'

Prayer

Most merciful Father,
    I confess that I have done little to promote your kingdom
    and advance your glory.
Pardon my shortcomings
    and give me greater enthusiasm in serving you.
Make me more ready and conscientious
    in my prayers, my giving and my example,
    to spread the knowledge of your truth
    and extend your kingdom;
    and may I do everything to your glory.
Amen.
William Walsham How (1823–1897)

Enlarging the picture

So what holds us back from sharing our faith, preventing us from freely and effectively identifying ourselves with Christ? We've already touched on some of the reasons, but there are others

25

besides, the very awkwardness we feel sometimes making it all the easier for other factors to get to work. If we're honest, we're frequently dying for an excuse to duck the issue, and it takes little to encourage us to walk away and leave the task of spreading the gospel to others. The scenarios that follow explore some of the reasons we may come up with for staying quiet, and ask whether it's time we grasped the nettle.

Scenario 1

Sharon spun round in astonishment as the car pulled out from the junction, straight into the path of an oncoming vehicle. It was obvious what was going to happen, a collision being inevitable, and so it proved, the two cars coming together with a sickening thud and shattering of glass. For a moment she stood transfixed, everything seeming to happen in slow motion, but then she hurried towards the stricken vehicles and peered inside. Incredibly there was no sign of blood, both drivers appearing dazed but otherwise unhurt.

'Are you all right?' said Sharon anxiously, looking again for signs of injury as the drivers emerged gingerly from the crumpled wreckage. They nodded blankly, more intent on surveying the damage than responding to her concern.

Sharon hesitated, caught in two minds. She knew she ought to stick around as a witness to the accident, but she was already late and was reluctant to get drawn in to what didn't finally concern her. What if one of the two men turned nasty, disputing her account of proceedings? What if she'd misunderstood what had happened, having failed perhaps to see a signal from one of the drivers? Anyway, why should *she* be the one to stick her neck out? There were plenty of others who'd seen what took place, many of whom could probably explain things as well as she could, if not better. That decided it. With a final look at the scene to ensure all was still well, she backed quietly away, quickening her pace as the wail of a distant siren reached her ears.

Discussion points

- If you found yourself in Sharon's position, what things would hold you back from telling of what you'd seen? How far do similar factors inhibit you from sharing your faith? What other concerns come into play in terms of witnessing to Christ?

- In what ways can we be eyewitnesses to the gospel? Does it make sense to speak in such terms? How should this shape our attempts to share our faith?

- If you've tried discussing your faith, have you ever found yourself drawn into more than you bargained for?

Scenario 2

'So then, lads,' said the PE teacher, 'which football team do you support?'

The hands shot up, each boy eager to affirm his allegiance.

'Man United, sir!'

'Me too, sir.'

'And me!'

'Liverpool, sir.'

'Arsenal.'

'Tottenham.'

'Chelsea.'

And so it continued, the big names trotted out time and again, regular as clockwork. Finally, they'd all spoken except for Callum, who sat fidgeting awkwardly, trying to avoid the teacher's eye. He knew what he wanted to say – Millham Town, his local non-league side – but he knew also what reaction he'd receive from his mates. They'd jeer as they always did, telling him it was time to support a *proper* team. Never mind that he watched every home game, whereas the closest any of them got to seeing their idols was on TV: local soccer simply wasn't cool.

'Callum,' prompted the teacher. You're very quiet. Haven't you a favourite?'

'Y . . . y . . . yes, sir,' stammered Callum, blushing furiously as his friends started to snigger. 'Mine's Man United too.'

The teacher looked disappointed. 'Shame,' he said. 'I was hoping one of you might say Millham Town. They're nothing special, granted, but they play some decent stuff at times. I watch them whenever I can and don't mind admitting it.'

Callum blushed yet deeper and pushed his Millham town scarf deeper into his kitbag, ashamed at having hidden where his true loyalties lay, but feeling it was too late now to go back on what he'd said.

Discussion points

- Have you have felt embarrassed about identifying yourself as a Christian? If so, why? Is this the same as being ashamed of Christ?

- Are there ways today in which you conceal your faith from others, or at least avoid allowing it to show too publicly?

- How do people respond to talk of faith? Are they interested in spirituality at all? Do they tar all religious beliefs with the same brush?

Scenario 3

The form teacher sighed as he ploughed his way through the collection of essays. He'd asked the pupils to write about what they thought of a book they were studying, but he was experienced enough to know that most of what he'd read so far had been cribbed off the Internet or plucked from a textbook. Not that he objected to a bit of background research but he could see that whole sentences, even paragraphs, had repeatedly been copied word for word, each essay little more than a mishmash of collected quotations.

Wearily he brandished the red pen and circled yet another suspect section, adding a curt remark at the foot of the page before turning to the final offering in the collection. It wasn't the best piece of writing by a long way, the grammar causing him to wince or smile in turns, but there was something about this essay that set it apart, marginally restoring his faith in the value of teaching. Here was what he'd been after. Rough and ready though it was, it carried the hallmark of authenticity, sustaining his interest throughout. 'Excellent work!' he scribbled happily at the bottom of the final page; then added, with a flourish, 'Your words made the book come alive!'

Discussion points

- Have you experienced people knocking on your door attempting to 'convert' you? How did you respond to them? Does anything attract you in what they do and say? Does anything irritate or alienate you?

- Have you ever tried sharing your faith? If so, how did you approach it? Did you try to give a potted summary of the gospel, or did you talk simply about what faith means to you? Which did you find most effective?

- Is speaking from the heart more important than learning some kind of technique in evangelism, or will we simply blunder about if we attempt this; ultimately getting nowhere?

Scenario 4

Few conversion stories are more dramatic than that of John Newton, celebrated above all for his great hymn 'Amazing grace' but the writer of many other classics besides, including 'Glorious things of thee are spoken', 'How sweet the name of Jesus sounds', 'One there is above all other' and 'Begone, unbelief'. Pressed into service as a midshipman with the Royal Navy in 1743, he went on, after being flogged for desertion, to serve with a slave ship, during which time, by his own admission, he sank into a dissolute life of 'misery and wretchedness'. Five years later, however, a fierce storm blew up while he was sailing home, and the very real prospect of death caused Newton to reappraise his life, to the point of surrendering his life to Christ there and then. His subsequent opposition to the slave trade was just one sign of a complete turn-around in his lifestyle, a transformation evidenced again in 1764 when he was ordained as a deacon and priest, serving at Olney in Buckinghamshire and later at St Mary Woolnoth, London, where he continued until his death in 1807.

Newton composed his own epitaph, which reads as follows: 'John Newton, clerk, once an infidel and a libertine, a servant of slaves in Africa, was by the rich mercy of our Lord and Saviour Jesus Christ, preserved, restored, pardoned and appointed to preach the Faith he had long laboured to destroy.'

Discussion points

- Newton was deeply conscious of the difference God had made to his life and burned with a longing to share it. What difference has God made to your life? Do you feel able to talk about it to others?

- Do you see sharing your faith as an essential part of disciple-ship? Do you tend to leave it to others?

- What are the chief obstacles to speaking about Christ today?

Food for thought

Consider the following proverbs and quotations. What are they saying? Which do you find most helpful? What are their strengths and weaknesses? Do you agree or disagree with the point they're making?

- Those having torches will pass them on to others. (Greek proverb)

- It is very important to live your faith by confessing it, and one of the best ways to confess it is to preach it. (Thomas Merton)

- Your love has a broken wing if it cannot fly across the sea. (Maltbie D. Babcock)

- Cry the gospel with your whole life. (Charles de Foucauld)

- Humble and self-forgetting we must be always, but diffident and apologetic about the gospel never. (James S. Stewart)

- Our task as laymen is to live our personal communion with Christ with such intensity as to make it contagious. (Paul Tournier)

- The reason some folks don't believe in mission is that the brand of religion they have isn't worth propagating. (Anon)

- The gospel is neither a discussion nor a debate. It is an announcement. (Paul S. Rees)

- The world is far more ready to receive the gospel than Christians are to hand it out. (George W. Peters)

- The gospel was not good advice but good news. (William Ralph Inge)

- It is no use walking anywhere to preach unless we preach as we walk. (St Francis of Assisi)

- Witnessing is removing the various barriers of our self-love to allow Christ, living within us, to show himself to our neighbours. (Paul Frost)

Prayer

Lord Jesus Christ,
>   though you call us to be your witnesses to the ends of the earth,
>   too often our commitment is a private affair,
>   kept so firmly to ourselves
>   that even friends and family barely see it,
>   let alone anyone else.

You have given us a faith to share,
>   but we have kept it to ourselves.

Forgive us.

We have failed to speak for you –
>   to talk of *your* love and *our* faith.

We have kept quiet about all we have received,
>   the strength, guidance and mercy you unfailingly provide.

You have given us a faith to share,
>   but we have kept it to ourselves.

Forgive us.

We have failed to speak through who and what we are,
>   so few of our actions and so little of our character
>   testifying to your renewing love.

We have been reluctant to stand out in a crowd,
>   unwilling to make sacrifices,
>   wary of being misunderstood,
>   so, instead of being ambassadors, we have hidden our loyalties,
>   our discipleship as ineffectual as it is incognito.

You have given us a faith to share,
>   but we have kept it to ourselves.

Forgive us.

When opportunities come to declare our allegiance,
>   to speak out for good or stand up against evil,
>   to honour our beliefs or confirm our convictions,
>   to speak or act in your name,

help us to live our faith and to share it,
gladly, wisely and sensitively making you known,
through Jesus Christ our Lord.
Amen.

Completing the picture

Below are some biblical verses relating to mission and evangelism. Reflect on them quietly together and then discuss any further thoughts arising from them.

- You will receive power when the Holy Spirit comes upon you, and you will be my witnesses not just in Jerusalem but in all Judaea and Samaria, and to the very ends of the earth. (Acts 1:8)
- My overwhelming aim is to conclude my mission, bringing to completion the work that the Lord Jesus has entrusted to me, which is to proclaim the good news concerning God's grace. (Acts 20:24)
- Christ did not send me to baptise but to declare the gospel, and to do so simply rather than through using clever words or arguments, lest this should empty the cross of its power. We proclaim Christ crucified, an offence to the Jews and plain folly to others, but to those who have been called, whether Jews or Greeks, it is the message of Christ, the power and wisdom of God. (1 Corinthians 1:17, 23, 24)
- Anyone united with Christ is a new creation; the old self has passed away in its entirety; everything is made new. All of this has been accomplished by God, who made peace with us through Christ and who has entrusted us in turn with the message of reconciliation. In Christ, in other words, God reconciled the world to himself, no longer holding people's offences against them, and he has committed to us his healing and uniting word.

So then, given that God has chosen to make his appeal through us, we are ambassadors for Christ, and therefore we beg you on his behalf to be truly reconciled with him. (2 Corinthians 5:17-20)

Blessing

Loving God,
    speak again *to* us,
    that you may speak again *through* us,
    making known to others all you have done
    through Jesus Christ our Lord.
Amen.

Session 3
A joy that shows

Theme

As Christians we speak often of joy, but how far do our lives reinforce our words?

Opening prayer

Holy God,
    may the glories of your creation
    awaken my heart to beauty and song.
Dispel the wintry coldness of my heart
    by the incoming of your Spirit,
    that I may know your true joy.
Refine my soul by your Spirit,
    and make me more aware of the things of true worth.
Help me to hear your still small voice.
Amen.

J. H. Jowett (1864–1923)

Setting the scene

Give thanks joyfully to the Father, who has made it possible for you to share in the bequest of the saints in his kingdom of light. (Colossians 1:11b, 12)

Even though you haven't seen him, you love him; despite not yet being able to see him you believe in him and rejoice with an

35

inexpressible and wonderful joy, for you are obtaining the fruits of your faith, the salvation of your souls. (1 Peter 1:8, 9)

Activity

Take a look at the following message:

ISNT THERE A MIRACLE HERE   FIND OUT

I AM THE RESURRECTION AND THE LIFE

Can you rearrange the letters to spell out a different message altogether? (The answer is in the Appendix, at the back of the book.)

Talk together afterwards about the sort of change faith in Christ has made in your life.

Introduction

What words would your average person in the street use to describe Christians? I've no doubt they'd come up with a fair few, largely uncomplimentary, and somewhere among them I strongly suspect would be the label 'killjoy'. To a point that's inevitable, for some of the things Christians baulk at are integral to what others consider 'having a good time'. But that's by no means the whole story. In the past, the Church has earned the reputation of being stern, censorious, judgemental, more interested in imposing rules and regulations on people than in contributing to their happiness. And let's not imagine we're so very different, for which of us can honestly say that our faith or life radiates joy? Negative attitudes all too easily take a hold in us, poisoning relationships and shaping our personality for the worse. And far from being a source of joy, faith itself can become a chore or duty, our prayer, worship and service offered mechanically rather than from a living spark within. That's all a far cry from the picture painted in the following readings, just some of the many passages in Scripture concerned with the joy of knowing and loving God.

Exploring the Scriptures

Psalm 9:1, 2; 16:11; 30:11, 12; 63:5-7; 98:4-8; 4:6, 7; 137:6

Lord, I will exult in you wholeheartedly, telling of the marvellous things you have done. Because of you, Almighty God, I will sing for joy, I will sing praises. You reveal the way that leads to life, and your presence overwhelms me with joy, bringing pleasure that endures for ever. You have turned my tears into dancing; you have removed sackcloth from me and clothed me instead with joy, such that I sing your praise and cannot be silent. Lord God, I will always thank you! I am contented deep within, like someone who has enjoyed a sumptuous meal. When I lie awake at night, reflecting during the hours of darkness over all you have done, my mouth worships you, songs of joy on my lips, for you have helped me, encircling me in the shadow of your wings.

Let the whole earth make a joyful noise to the Lord, praising him with songs and cries of joy. Sing praise to the Lord. Play harp music, blow trumpets and horns, shout for joy to our Lord and king. Let the sea roar and all creatures within it, the earth sing and all who live upon it likewise. Rivers, clap your hands, and hills sing for joy before the Lord.

Many ask in their prayers, 'Lord, grant us more blessings, look more kindly upon us,' but the joy you have given me, Lord, exceeds anything they will ever have, despite all their grain and wine. May I never be able to sing again if I forget you, if I fail to consider you my greatest joy!

John 15:9-11

I have loved you just as the Father loves me; remain in my love. You will remain in it if you obey my commandments, just as I have obeyed my Father's commandments and lived always in his love. The reason I tell you all this is that my joy may be in you, *your* joy thus being complete.

Prayer

O God, I know you love me!
My heart is all joy because of what you have done for me.
How good you have been to me, O God most high;
    in my joy I shall sing and delight.
I shall sing in your honour.
Amen.

Carmelite monastery, Quidenham

Enlarging the picture

What sort of joy, then, should we show as Christians? Faced with
the spectre of joyless discipleship I talked about earlier, there's a
danger of overcompensating and exhibiting an exaggerated
happiness that has little substance. To go back to the point made
earlier about how people see us, some of my non-Christian
friends have spoken, perhaps unfairly though not entirely without
grounds, of Christians wearing a grin like a Cheshire cat, the
smile a complete turn-off since it seems altogether false. Others
have been deterred by experiences of worship in which the
emphasis fell so heavily on celebration that there was no room for
anything else. The joy we are called to show as Christians is very
different, having more to do with inner contentment, a happiness
that can endure even through tears, a sense of peace and fulfil-
ment that, no matter what it comes up against, can never finally
be extinguished. Such joy is life-affirming and contagious, strik-
ing a chord in others and leaving them not feeling judged and
found wanting but encountered and found to be of value. It
speaks for itself, testifying to new life in Christ in a way words
can never begin to. Is that what people see in you? It should be, at
least in part. Imperfect though we are, there should be at least

something about us that gives others a glimpse of the joy they too can share in Christ. The following scenarios explore this from four different perspectives, each leading on to points for discussion:

Scenario 1

Matt leant across the desk and nudged his colleague, Petra. 'Have you seen the boss today?' he said.

Petra grinned broadly, eyes raised in acknowledgement. 'Yeah, it's amazing – like he's a different guy.'

'You're telling me,' said Matt. 'He usually takes my head off when he walks in, but today he was all smiles – almost like he was pleased to see me.'

'Whoa, steady now!' laughed Petra. 'Let's not go too far.'

'It's true, though,' said Matt. 'I've never seen such a change. He seems so happy, so at peace with himself. I just can't think what's come over him.'

Petra cupped her hand over her mouth and bent low across the desk. 'The word from personnel is that he's got religion.'

'Never!' gasped Matt.

'That's what they're saying.'

'And do you think it's true?'

Petra shrugged. 'Can't say for sure, but Betty in Accounts reckons she saw him coming out of church last Sunday.'

'Well, who'd have thought it?'

'I know, *him* of all people!'

'Can't say I go in for all that God stuff myself,' said Matt.

'No, nor me, but I tell you what: if he's still as different next week as he is now, I'll start to wonder if perhaps there's something in it after all.'

Discussion points

• How would you describe joy? Is it the same thing as happiness? What does our joy as Christians rest on?

- Have you met people whose lives seem to have been completely changed and who radiate a kind of inner joy? What is it about them that catches your attention?

- Do you feel the same sense of joy that you once did? If not, why? Is it down to what life has thrown at you, or have you lost sight of the essentials of the gospel?

Scenario 2

Sophie and Tony settled themselves self-consciously into their pew, making space between them for their two children. This was their first time at church and they weren't sure what to expect, but a leaflet through the door had caught their attention and they'd decided to give it a try. Already, though, they'd a feeling things weren't right, a middle-aged couple having glared at them as if they'd no right to be sitting where they were, and then shuffling officiously into the row of seats in front.

The service started and before long the two boys grew restless, fidgeting and playing with their toys. Tony reached forward to quieten them, but as he did so the woman in front turned with a frown, tutting and shaking her head. Tony recoiled, angry and embarrassed.

Subdued for a time, the boys sat quietly save for the occasional whisper, but as they rose for a hymn one fumbled his hymnbook and it fell crashing to the floor. Heads turned again, several this time, disapproval in every eye.

Sophie and Tony shuffled awkwardly, not enjoying this experience at all. 'If you want joy, real joy . . .' ran the hymn, but from what they'd seen so far there was little of that on offer here. A sudden movement caught Sophie's eye, and a bag was thrust in front of her. She looked round, puzzled, then heard the clink of coins and realised she was meant to contribute to the collection.

'Tony,' she whispered, nudging her partner in the ribs, 'did you bring any change?'

Tony rummaged hurriedly in his pockets, the steward standing by impatiently. 'I think so,' he said. 'Won't be a tick. Ah yes, here.' He brandished a pound coin, but too late; the steward had given up and walked away, the hapless couple left grinning sheepishly as all eyes fastened on them once again.

It was the first time they visited church. It was also the last.

Discussion points

• How far would you say that joy characterises your local church? How far should it?

• How far does joy characterise *you*? Do you think joy should be a distinguishing characteristic of Christians, and, if so, in what ways should it show itself?

• Why do you think Christians are seen sometimes as killjoys? Has the Church been guilty on occasions of focusing on negatives at the cost of positives? If so, in what way? Do you make the same mistake at times in your own life?

Scenario 3

Florence lifted herself painfully from her chair in answer to the doorbell. It was a gruelling business, even this normally routine act a marathon, her arthritis so severe that every movement was an effort, bringing tears to her eyes, but gingerly she inched herself into a standing position. 'Won't be a moment,' she called cheerfully. She would be, though – considerably more than a moment – but the caller was aware of her condition and happy to wait.

Florence reached for her walking frame, feeling out tentatively towards the wall. Her sight had been failing for years, all that was left to her being a tiny patch of peripheral vision in one eye, but finally her hand felt the reassuring support of the Zimmer, and she shuffled patiently across the room. Halfway, she paused, wearied by the exertion, age having taken a heavy toll on her frail body.

A worried voice through the letterbox stirred her back into action. 'Are you all right, Florence?'

'Yes, dear, almost with you.'

Another tortuous shuffle, and then twisted fingers struggled with the latch, before she finally prised open the door.

'Hello, Florence. I was worried for a moment. How are you today?'

'Me?' she said, with a radiant smile that lit up the street. 'Oh I'm fine.'

Discussion points

- Florence wasn't her real name, but the woman above was one I visited many times during my time in the pastoral ministry. Whether those visits did her any good I cannot say, but they were always a tonic to me, and I invariably came away from them humbled, inspired and moved by her astonishing cheerfulness in such adversity. Do you know of similar people? What is the secret of their joy?

- Do you think you could still feel joy in times of adversity? Is adversity the greatest threat to joy or are other factors more likely to undermine it? What might these be?

- According to Hebrews 12:2, Jesus endured death on a cross 'for the joy set before him'. How far, then, is joy as a Christian rooted in the present and how far does it depend on the future God holds in store?

Scenario 4

The story of Mother Teresa is well known, but perhaps what's less publicised is the joy associated with her ministry. According, however, to Malcolm Muggeridge, who wrote of her and the order she founded in his book *Something Beautiful for God*, this was their defining characteristic. 'I never met such delightful, happy women, or such an atmosphere of joy as they create. Mother Teresa, as she is fond of explaining, attaches the utmost importance to this joyousness. The poor, she says, deserve not just service and dedication, but also the joy that belongs to human love.' Mother Teresa herself described the life of abstinence she lived as one of 'joyful freedom', and it was that inner joy, coupled with the warmth and sincerity of her love, that left its indelible mark on all who met her.

Discussion points

- Is your response to God, whether in worship or service, joyful or grudging?

- How can we cultivate joyousness?

- How far would you see bringing joy to others as a summary of what being a Christian is all about? How far do you think you succeed in doing that?

Food for thought

Consider the following proverbs and quotations. What are they saying? Which do you find most helpful? What are their strengths and weaknesses? Do you agree or disagree with the point they're making?

- The sweet mark of a Christian is not faith, or even love, but joy. (Samuel M. Shoemaker)

- Joy is the most infallible sign of the presence of God. (Leon Bloy)

- Joy is the echo of God's life within us. (Joseph Marmion)

- If you have no joy in your religion, there's a leak in your Christianity somewhere. (W. A. Sunday)

- It is always springtime in the heart that loves God. (St John Vianney)

- We are all strings in the concert of his joy. (Jakob Boehme)

- When you're smiling, the whole world smiles with you. (From the song by Mark Fisher, Joe Goodwin and Larry Shay)

- A smile costs nothing. (Traditional)

- Joy is the serious business of heaven. (C. S. Lewis)

- When I think upon my God, my heart is so full of joy that the notes dance and leap from my pen; and since God has given me a cheerful heart, it will be pardoned me that I serve him with a cheerful spirit. (Franz Josef Haydn)

- One joy dispels a hundred cares. (Oriental proverb)

- God is infinite fun. (Mary O'Hara)

- Happiness is not a state to arrive at, but a manner of travelling. (Margaret Lee Runbeck)

- Laugh, and the world laughs with you; weep, and you weep alone. (Ella Wheeler Wilcox)

- A contented mind is a continual feast. (English proverb)

- Joy is distinctly a Christian word and a Christian thing. It . . . has its springs deep down inside, and that spring never runs dry, no matter what happens. Only Jesus gives that joy. He had joy, singing its music deep within, even under the shadow of the cross. (Samuel Gordon)

- The joy that Jesus gives is the result of our disposition being at one with his own disposition. (Oswald Chambers)

- God cannot give us happiness and peace apart from himself, because it is not there. There is no such thing. (C. S. Lewis)

Prayer

We have tasted joy, Lord,
    moments when our hearts danced with delight
    and our spirits leapt within us,
    but they were the exception rather than the rule,
    isolated moments instead of an ongoing experience.
Too often faith has been arid and sombre,
    concerned with negatives instead of positives,
    losing sight of all you have given to celebrate.
So, we pray,
    touch our lives afresh,
    and may your joy shape every part.

Though we are faced by problems,
    anxieties that hang heavy upon us,
    difficulties that encumber and undermine,
    touch our lives afresh,
    and may your joy shape every part.

Though we are faced by routine,
    mundane demands, chores and responsibilities
    that sap the spirit
    and shrink our horizons,
    touch our lives afresh,
    and may your joy shape every part.

Though we are faced by sorrow,
    tasting the bitterness of tears,
    the pain of grief, loss, hurt, or despair,
    touch our lives afresh,
    and may your joy shape every part.

Whatever we have been through,
    whatever we experience
    whatever the future may hold,

touch our lives afresh,
and may your joy shape every part.
Amen.

Completing the picture

Below are some biblical verses reminding us once again of the centrality of joy in the Christian life. Reflect on them quietly together and then discuss any further thoughts arising from them.

- Worship the Lord joyfully; come before him with songs of praise. (Psalm 100:2)

- The angel said to them, 'Have no fear. I come with good news for you – news that will bring great joy to all people.' (Luke 2:10)

- The disciples there brimmed over with joy and the Holy Spirit. (Acts 13:52)

- Now may God, the spring of hope, fill you completely with joy and peace in believing, so that hope may flourish within you, through the power of the Holy Spirit. (Romans 15:13)

- The Spirit, in contrast, generates love, joy, peace, patience, compassion, goodness and faithfulness. (Galatians 5:22)

Blessing

Life-giving God,
    may the good news of your love
    colour each moment of every day,
    nourishing us with a joy deep within
    that both attracts and transmits itself to others,
    speaking unmistakably of you.
Amen.

Session 4
A concern that shows

Theme

Jesus calls us to love our neighbour as ourselves, but is there anything distinctive in the care or concern we as Christians show to others?

Opening prayer

I bring before you, O Lord,
   the troubles and perils of people and nations,
   the pain of prisoners and captives,
   the sorrows of the bereaved,
   the needs of strangers,
   the vulnerability of the weak,
   the downheartedness of the weary,
   the diminishing powers of the aged.
O Lord, draw near to each,
   for the sake of Jesus Christ our Lord.
Amen.

St Anselm (1033–1109)

Setting the scene

Let us show concern for each other, doing what we can to display love and show kindness. Never forget to do good or to help one another, for it is sacrifices such as these that are pleasing to God. (Hebrews 10:24; 13:16)

If we have plenty, yet see others in need and shut our hearts to them, how can we claim to love God? Little children, do not let love be simply all talk, but instead let us show its authenticity in action. (1 John 3:17, 18)

Activity

Changing just one letter at a time, and making an accepted word every time, can you turn each of the words in the top row to the corresponding word underneath? (Answers are given in the Appendix in the back of the book, but you may be able to find a faster way of doing each than I've come up with.)

POOR	SELF	TAKE	HURT	GREED
RICH	CARE	GIVE	HEAL	SHARE

Talk briefly together about how far Christians should, and actually do, help make a difference to the lives of others.

Introduction

We spoke in the first session of loving others, but the discussion there was largely in the abstract, concerned, if you like, with loving attitudes in general. In this session we explore in more detail the implications of love in action, through what we might variously describe as concern, compassion, kindness or service. The Church has a chequered history in this context: on the one hand it has been involved in all kinds of social reform and community involvement, never mind the innumerable acts of untold individuals, but on the other it has focused too much at times on faith rather than works and been so concerned with people's spiritual needs that it has overlooked the material. It's certainly true we can't earn God's approval, but that shouldn't lead us to underestimate the importance of how we live, for, according to Jesus, faith necessarily shows itself in action and, above all, in a concern for others. In the following passages, as in the two earlier, are reminders of just how important that is.

Exploring the Scriptures

James 2:14-17

What good is it, my brothers and sisters, if you claim to have faith but fail to show it in works? Can faith save you? If a brother or sister is naked and lacks sufficient food, and one of you says to them, 'Go in peace, keep warm and eat plenty,' but fails to give them what they really need, what value is there in that? Mark my words, faith alone, without works, is dead.

Matthew 25:31-40

When the Son of Man comes in his glory, together with his angels, he will sit in state on his throne, with all the nations gathered before him, and he will separate people one from the other as a shepherd separates the sheep from the goats, putting the sheep to his right and the goats to his left. Then the king will say to those on his right, 'Come, those whom my Father has blessed – inherit the kingdom prepared for you from the foundation of the world. I was hungry and you gave me something to eat, thirsty and you gave me a drink, a stranger and you made me welcome, naked and you clothed me, sick and you visited me, in prison and you had time for me.' Then the righteous will answer, 'Lord, when did we see you hungry and give you food, or thirsty and give you a drink? When did we see you a stranger and make you welcome, or naked and clothe you? When was it that we saw you sick or in prison and visited you?' Then the king will answer, 'I tell you the truth, whenever you did it to the least of your brothers and sisters, you did it also to me.'

Prayer

Watch, dear Lord,
    with those who wake, or watch, or weep tonight,
    and give your angels charge over those who sleep.
Tend your sick ones, O Lord Christ,
    rest your weary ones,
    bless your dying ones,
    soothe your suffering ones,
    pity your afflicted ones,
    shield your joyous ones,
    all for your love's sake.
Amen.
St Augustine of Hippo (354–430)

Enlarging the picture

So, then, what service do you offer to others? I've no doubt you do something, perhaps volunteering help to a friend or neighbour, perhaps giving to various charities, perhaps even being involved somehow in your local community, but are you doing as much as you could or should be? Time and again I personally have felt put to shame by the example of non-Christians, the generosity with which they give of their time, money, skills and energy far exceeding anything I offer myself. Admittedly our resources and the demands made upon them are all different, so there can be no one-size-fits-all recommendation as to what we should or shouldn't be doing, but if we take seriously those words of Jesus, that in serving others we serve him, can we ever be content to rest on our laurels? Definitely not! Our faith should show itself in commitment to others and a lifestyle that shows we care. The following scenarios, each leading on to points for discussion, explore some of the ways we might do that.

Scenario 1

'What did you do with that charity appeal letter?' called Katherine.

'Oh,' said Andy, as he re-entered the room, 'I threw it away. Didn't think you'd want to bother with it this time. We gave something last year, remember.'

Katherine nodded. 'Yes, I know. It's just that I caught the first paragraph and couldn't help feeling we should do something more.'

'We *do* give to other charities,' Andy reminded her, clearly wishing to drop the matter. 'Don't you think we're doing enough already?'

'I guess so, but I can't get those images out of my mind: all those hungry people and sick children, so many dying every day.'

'It gets to me too, you know,' snapped Andy, 'but what can we do? They say most of the money gets siphoned off by governments or swallowed up in admin. I'm not sure sometimes if there's any point giving at all.'

'But is that just an excuse,' persisted Katherine, 'a way people can duck the issue? And even if there's truth in it, does that mean we shouldn't even try to help?'

Andy shrugged. 'Probably not,' he admitted. 'But I ask you, they were asking for a regular donation of £5 a month. I don't mind giving a one-off but, be reasonable, we just can't afford that sort of commitment. We're due to change the car soon, remember, and then there's the holidays to think about, decorating the house, the Sky subscription, never mind the rest. Why don't we wait till we've got a bit more ready money and discuss it again then?'

Katherine sighed, defeated for the moment but unconvinced.

Discussion points

- How often do you take note of charity appeals? How often do you ignore them?

- Which charities are most likely to elicit your support, and why? Do you support any regularly? Do you take a genuine interest in their work?

- What excuses do people make for not giving? Have you used these excuses yourself? Are they genuine reasons, or just that – excuses?

Scenario 2

Mike wavered for a moment, then put the jar of coffee into his trolley and moved down the aisle. He'd been torn for a moment, unsure whether to go for the fair-trade alternative rather than his favourite brand, a Christian Aid poster he'd seen that week having pricked his conscience. Once more, though, he'd gone for his preferred choice – not, he told himself, because it was cheaper but simply because the other didn't taste anywhere near as good.

He reached the fruit section and paused, conscience stirred again as he reached for a bargain pack of bananas. Scruples urged one thing, inclinations another, Mike – despite what he liked to pretend – never liking to pay more than he needed. Would going for the fair-trade option really make a difference? Who could say for sure how much the growers actually received for their product? And anyway, hadn't he heard somewhere that the free market economy was the only way to true prosperity for all? Furtively, almost as though he were a shoplifter, he dropped a bargain pack into his trolley and continued with his shopping. But it was no good: he couldn't silence that little voice within. Maybe his efforts wouldn't achieve much in the grand scheme of things, but they were a start, if nothing else, and, who could say, together with those of others perhaps they might make a difference after all.

He hurried back, swapping the bananas for a fair-trade pack, and then the jar of coffee caught his eye once more. 'Shall I?' he wondered, wrestling with himself once again in an agony of indecision. 'I suppose I could give it one more try . . .'

Discussion points

- We're increasingly told today that our responsibility towards others – especially towards the world's poor and future generations – involves examining our lifestyle and changing where necessary. What changes do you see as important?

- What changes do you find it hardest to make? What factors hold you back?

- What initiatives do you know of designed to promote greater justice in trade or more responsible stewardship of the environment?

Scenario 3

Claire groaned as the shrill tone of the telephone shattered the tranquillity of the moment. It had been an exhausting week, the pressures of work, never mind of running the home, having been particularly demanding, and she was just about all in. Only the prospect of a relaxing weekend away from it all had kept her going – the chance to put her feet up and enjoy a well-earned break. Understandably, then, this late-night call filled her with foreboding. People didn't usually ring so late, so who could it be? Almost certainly it meant bad news or someone wanting a favour. She picked up the receiver, bracing herself for the worst.

'Hello, Claire,' came a voice, 'sorry to ring at this time of night, but I'm wondering if you could help us out.' It was her friend Alicia, and Claire had a sinking feeling about what was coming next.

'It's the kids; we don't know what to do with them. Brian's mum's been taken into hospital, you see – seems like she's really bad – and we've been told to get there as soon as possible. It wouldn't be fair to take the children – not all that way – so we desperately need someone to have them for the weekend. I know it's a lot to ask, but I can't think who else to turn to.'

Claire did her best to hide the note of dismay in her voice. 'I see . . . er . . . well . . . are you sure there's no one else?'

'No one, honestly. *Please*, Claire, Brian's beside himself with worry.'

There was no escape. But, even as that truth sank home, Claire felt ashamed. Alicia was her friend, after all, and someone she'd personally introduced to her local church just a few months previously. What sort of impression was her lukewarm response putting across?

'Of course I'll help, Alicia – isn't that what friends are for? I'll pick them up first thing tomorrow, shall I?'

There was an awkward pause at the other end of the line, before Alicia hesitantly continued. 'Actually, Claire, I was hoping you could come *now*, so that we can make a start immediately.

Now! Claire almost keeled over in disbelief, but somehow she put on a voice of calm assurance. 'No problem, Alicia. I'll leave straightaway. Give me twenty minutes and I'll be with you.'

Discussion points

- 'A friend in need is a friend indeed.' What acts of friendship have meant the most to you?

- What would your first thoughts have been in Claire's shoes?

- Do we sometimes use giving to causes, whether at home or abroad, as an excuse to ignore needs closer to home?

Scenario 4

Mention serving others and many of us will automatically think of Mother Teresa, our example of joy in the previous session – but there are others who have shown similar commitment, among them the celebrated theologian, clergyman, philosopher and musician, Albert Schweitzer. In 1896, aged just 21, he came to a bold and selfless decision, resolving to focus on his academic career in science and art for the next nine years and then to devote the rest of his life to the service of humanity. This he duly did, studying medicine in 1905 and then, after qualifying as a doctor, setting up a hospital in Lambaréné, Africa, dedicated to treating sufferers from leprosy and sleeping sickness. During the rest of his life he was to treat thousands of people, giving all his money to support and maintain the hospital, as well as tirelessly raising funds for it. Schweitzer didn't just talk about faith – he demonstrated it in action, dedicating his time, skills, energy and resources to the service of others. To him, quite simply, this was what faith is all about.

Discussion points

- The Church has been accused in the past of being preoccupied with people's spiritual needs and forgetting the physical. Is that a fair assessment? What relative emphasis would you place on these?

- Is faith without works any faith at all? Are works without faith to be preferred?

- What could you be doing, individually and as a church, to serve those around you?

Food for thought

Consider the following proverbs and quotations. What are they saying? Which do you find most helpful? What are their strengths and weaknesses? Do you agree or disagree with the point they're making?

- To give pleasure to a single heart by a single kind act is better than a thousand head-bowings in prayer. (Saadi)

- The purpose of human life is to serve and to show compassion and the will to help others. (Albert Schweitzer)

- Happiness is not perfected until it is shared. (Jane Porter)

- No man can be a friend of Jesus Christ who is not a friend to his neighbour. (Robert H. Benson)

- He alone loves the Creator perfectly who manifests a pure love for his neighbour. (The Venerable Bede)

- If we do not help a man in trouble, it is as if we caused the trouble. (Nachman of Bratslav)

- Kindness gives birth to kindness. (Sophocles)

- When a man has compassion for others, God has compassion for him. (The Talmud)

- The love of our neighbour is the only door out of the dungeon of self. (George Macdonald)

- Kindness is the golden chain by which society is bound together. (Goethe)

- Man is never nearer the Divine than in his compassionate moments. (Joseph H. Hertz)

- Kindness has converted more sinners than zeal, eloquence and learning. (Frederick W. Faber)

- I sought my soul, the soul I could not see.
  I sought my God and God eluded me.
  I sought my brother and found all three. (Anon)

Prayer

We have talked of service, Lord,
    of self-sacrifice and costly commitment,
    of putting the needs of others before our own,
    but so often it's only words,
    exposed as hollow through our actions.
Teach us to practise what we preach –
    truly to live out our faith.

We have been slow to respond when we could have helped,
    slow to offer encouragement, support,
    a shoulder to lean on,
    an understanding word or gesture of kindness,
    a little of our time, skills or money in the service of others.
Teach us to practise what we preach –
    truly to live out our faith.

We have shut out the cries of the poor,
    turning our backs on the suffering and injustice of this world,
    preferring to pretend that all is well
    rather than face up to our responsibilities
    or change our lifestyle.
Teach us to practise what we preach –
    truly to live out our faith.

We have called you Lord,
    but overlooked your call in the plight of a neighbour,
    the despair of the hungry,
    the groans of the sick,
    the pleas of the oppressed
    and the anguish of the sorrowful,
    yet whenever *we* are in need
    we expect you instantly to hear and respond.
Teach us to practise what we preach –
    truly to live out our faith.

Give us all a gentle heart,
  a caring heart,
  a compassionate heart –
  a heart so full of you that it beats with your love
  and sends it coursing out to all.
Teach us to practise what we preach –
  truly to live out our faith.
Amen.

Completing the picture

Below are some biblical verses speaking of the need to show our faith in action. Reflect on them quietly together and then discuss any further thoughts arising from them.

- Do good whenever possible to those who need it. (Proverbs 3:27)

- Bear one another's burdens, and so fulfil the law of Christ. We should seize the chance, whenever it presents itself, to do good to everyone, especially to those belonging to the household of faith. (Galatians 6:2, 10)

- Be renewed deep within, mind and soul, putting on the new self created in the likeness of God, in righteousness, holiness and truth. Be thoughtful and compassionate in all your dealings with each other, showing forgiveness just as God has done to you in Christ. (Ephesians 4:23, 24, 32)

Blessing

Loving God,
  go with us that we may go with you;
  work *in* us that we may work *for* you,
  responding to *you* through serving *others*.
Amen.

Session 5
A faith that shows

Theme

Faith is not about having all the answers, but about trusting God and committing our lives to him. How far, as Christians, do we actually do that?

Opening prayer

Lord God,
   I am no longer my own, but yours.
Put me to what you will,
   rank me with whom you will.
Put me to doing, put me to enduring;
   let me be employed for you
   or laid aside for you,
   exalted for you
   or brought low for you;
   let me be full,
   let me be empty;
   let me have all things,
   let me have nothing.
I freely and wholeheartedly yield all things
   to your pleasure and disposal.
And now, glorious and blessed God,
   Father, Son and Holy Spirit,
   you are mine and I am yours.
So be it.
Amen.

Charles Wesley (1707–1788)

Setting the scene

Whatever happens, conduct yourselves in a manner befitting the gospel of Christ, so that, whether I come to see you for myself or only hear reports concerning you in my absence, I will know that you stand resolute in one spirit, striving together with a common purpose for the faith of the gospel. (Philippians 1:27)

Try harder than ever, then, my friends, to ensure that God's call and election is an ongoing reality; do that and you will not stumble in faith. (2 Peter 1:10)

Activity

Take a look at the following:

Which of the central circles is the biggest?

Which of the central dots is the lightest?

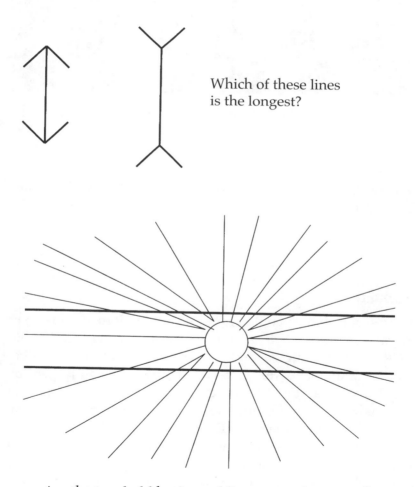

Which of these lines
is the longest?

Are the two bold horizontal lines curved or straight?

61

How about here: are the lines curved or straight?

Talk honestly together afterwards about how far people see any difference in our lives as Christians.

Introduction

If there's one thing people crave in our modern world, apart perhaps from love, it's a sense of purpose, a belief that life has some kind of meaning beyond the ups and downs of our all-too-fleeting mortal span. Are we and our universe simply here by chance? Are we destined to flicker for a moment on the stage of time, only to be extinguished for ever? Some feel precisely that, and in consequence their life is overshadowed by a profound sense of emptiness. Of course, not everyone feels the same, and it would be intensely patronising to suggest otherwise, but many yearn to fill that aching void within, to find a creed or conviction that gives substance to who and what they are.

Does Christianity provide the answer? For some, yes, the Church offering spiritual guidance and sustenance, but others are less sure. Why? Partly, I think, there's an issue with religion *per se*, many seeing it as responsible for a divided world in which a fanatical few see suicide and slaughter as a sacred duty. Others are put off by heavy-handed proselytising, a foot-in-the-door approach that seeks to impose itself on others, not least when it finds them at their lowest ebb. Others again are troubled by questions, wanting to believe but unable to reconcile doubts with traditional doctrine. Still others are disenchanted by nominal Christianity, the kind of faith that is all too obviously superficial, making little if any difference to the way people live.

True faith, I believe, is different from any of these. It doesn't claim to have all the answers. It doesn't thrust itself on others. It doesn't alienate and destroy, nor is it a going through the motions. Instead it is simple yet profound, resting not on doctrinal soundness but on personal experience and involving not just the mind but, above all, the heart. It has room for questions and can wrestle with doubt, yet still shine with a quiet inner light. Never the finished product, it is always in the making – growing, evolving and responding. Humble enough to admit its deficiencies, open enough to learn from others yet strong enough to face all, such faith needs no trumpet to broadcast its credentials – it speaks for itself.

In the following two readings we get a taste of such faith.

Exploring the Scriptures

John 20:19, 20, 24-29

That Sunday evening found the disciples huddled together behind locked doors, terrified of the Jewish authorities. All of a sudden Jesus appeared and stood among them, saying, 'Peace be with you,' upon which he showed them his hands and side, and the disciples, recognising the Lord, were overcome with joy.

However, one of their number, Thomas (otherwise known as the Twin), wasn't with them, so when the disciples told him, 'We've seen the Lord!' he retorted, 'I won't believe that unless I not only see the nail marks in his hands and the wound in his side but also place my fingers in them.'

The following week the disciples were again assembled indoors, only this time Thomas was with them. Once more, despite the door being locked, Jesus appeared and stood among them, uttering the same words: 'Peace be with you.' 'Put your finger here,' he said to Thomas, 'and see my hands. Reach out your hand and place it in my side. Let's have no more doubting: believe!' Thomas answered him, 'My Lord and my God!' whereupon Jesus responded, 'Have you believed because you have seen me? Happy are those, I tell you, who come to believe even though they have not seen.'

Colossians 1:3-6; 2:5-7

We always thank God, the Father of our Lord Jesus Christ, because we have heard of your faith and your love for all the saints, springing from the hope stored up for you in heaven that you heard about in the word of truth, the gospel that has come to you. Just as it has been bearing fruit and growing in the whole world, so, from the moment you first heard it and truly understood the grace of God, it has been bearing fruit among you.

I cannot be with you in body, but I'm present in spirit, and am greatly heartened by the way you unwaveringly stand together in your faith in Christ. So then, having received him as Lord, continue to dwell in Christ, rooted and growing in him, established in the faith taught to you, and overflowing with thanksgiving.

Prayer

Behold, Lord, an empty vessel that needs to be filled.
My Lord, fill it.
I am weak in faith; strengthen me.
I am cold in love; warm me and make me fervent
    that my love may go out to my neighbour.
I do not have a strong and firm faith;
    at times I doubt and am unable to trust you altogether.
O Lord,
    help me and strengthen my faith and trust in you.
Amen.

Martin Luther (1483–1546)

Enlarging the picture

What sort of things, then, does faith entail? Can it really stand alongside doubt, admitting room for questions, or is the point of Thomas' story above that these must all be resolved if we would truly believe? Is it relevant to the world as we experience and live it today? Can it really answer our deepest needs, giving shape and direction to our lives? And can it make an impression on others, speaking to them of a vibrant, life-giving experience that they in turn want to share? The following scenarios open up some of those questions, exploring both the challenges faith must face and the answers it can give. As always, each leads on to points for discussion:

Scenario 1

'OK, if God loves us so much, why does he allow so many to suffer, tell me that?'

'I can't,' said Fred. 'I wish I could, heaven knows, but I don't understand, and that's the truth of it.'

'All right then, if God exists, where is he? And don't give me any of that "spirit" nonsense.'

'Honestly, Harold, I've no choice. I don't know exactly what it means, but with God we're talking about something different from flesh and blood, different from anything words were designed for. Spirit's about the best we can do. He's here, there, everywhere.'

'Is that right?' sneered Harold. 'So how does he *hear* people – *see* them? Has he got ears and eyes?'

Fred shrugged. 'I don't know.'

'There's not much you *do* know, is there?'

'I know *this*: that God loves me and will go on loving me always.'

Harold snorted in derision. 'I suppose you mean by that even beyond death?'

'Yes.'

'And just how are you meant to come back to life after you're dead and gone?'

'I've no idea. It's down to faith, eventually.'

'Is that the best you can do?' said Harold. 'I thought you Christians are meant to have all the answers.'

Fred smiled. 'It's you who say that, not me. I've got as many doubts as the next person – all kinds of things that bug me. But I still believe God cares and can do more than I can ever get my head round. I can't prove it; it's just something I feel deep inside. Though I can't put it into words, it's real to me, and it could be real for you too if only you'd see past the questions and learn to live with them instead.'

Harold shook his head. 'I won't believe while there are still things I don't understand.'

'Then you'll never believe at all,' sighed Fred, 'for there will always be those.'

Discussion points

- Are there aspects of life and faith that you find hard to reconcile? How would you have answered Harold's questions in the scenario above? Could you have come up with better answers?

- Is appealing to faith a way of burying our heads in the sand and avoiding awkward issues, or is it ultimately the only answer we can give? How can we avoid the charge of blind faith? On what is faith rooted?

- Do you feel threatened by questions or do they help deepen your faith? Do you see doubt as a part of faith or as its opposite?

Scenario 2

The prisoner gazed at the chaplain, and then buried his face in his hands. 'I want to believe, God knows, but how can I? I killed a man, didn't I? Left a woman without her husband and two kids without their dad. How can anyone be forgiven for that?'

'You *can*,' said the chaplain, 'or at least you can if you're truly sorry.'

But the prisoner shook his head. 'No, it's not possible, not for someone like me. I'm a worthless nobody, a waste of space – that's what people tell me.'

'You're wrong, despite what others may say. Everyone matters to God, whoever they are. Of course he doesn't condone what you've done – not for a moment – and I've no doubt it will haunt you for the rest of your days, but *he* can forgive and forget even if *you* can't.'

'It's too late for that.'

'It's never too late. With his help you can start again.'

'Do you *really* believe that?' said the prisoner, looking deep into the chaplain's eyes. The chaplain looked away, unable to hold the man's gaze. 'Not always,' he confessed, 'no. But I *try* to, and *want* to, and I believe God wants me to as well. Not everyone will give you a second chance, you know that as well as me, but *he* will – a second, third and fourth if necessary, however many it takes. Don't judge him by me, though – check it out for yourself. That's the only way to find out. Go on, give it a try.'

Discussion points

- We talk as Christians about God being able to change things, but do you believe he can change those who've gone off the rails? Are there some people who you feel are beyond change? Does that say more about you than about God?

- Do you still believe God can change you? What makes that hard to believe? Do you find such faith as easy as you used to?

- Do you still believe the world can change? Again, what makes that hard to believe? What sort of things help to restore such faith?

Scenario 3

Joel shifted uneasily as the preacher wound up his sermon. His worst fear had been realised, and he was irritated.

'What's up?' whispered his wife. 'Bored?'

Bored! If only! He'd come hoping to be precisely that – to have his apathy vindicated, prejudice reinforced, comfortable status quo left undisturbed – but no, he wasn't bored, far from it. The words had hit home, every one of them – probing, challenging, unsettling, demanding a response – and try as he might he couldn't push them aside. He wanted to walk away as if nothing had happened, to go back to the familiar and reassuring routine, poking fun at religion with his mates as he'd done so often before. But he knew now that he couldn't, however hard he might try.

A tear pricked his eye and ran down his cheek – a curious mixture of sorrow and joy – and though he impatiently brushed it aside, another soon took its place. What had got into him, he wondered? He couldn't understand it. But he couldn't fight it either.

'It's *your* choice,' said the preacher, with a final flourish. 'Do you believe it or not? – you decide.'

'Oh I believe,' he murmured. 'I never thought I'd say it, but I really do believe.'

Discussion points

- In what ways have you felt God's call? Have there been times when it was unwelcome and you tried to resist it? Are you perhaps resisting his call even now?

- Does what you believe still stir your heart or has faith become mechanical, more about intellectual assent than joyful response? What sort of things can erode faith as the years go by?

- How can we keep faith fresh? What sort of things do you find most helpful in achieving this?

Scenario 4

The recent film *The Lion, the Witch and the Wardrobe* captured the public imagination, but equally dramatic in its own way was the spiritual journey of C. S. Lewis, the writer of the book on which the film is based. Raised by Christian parents, he showed fleeting interest in Christianity after his mother died while he was at boarding school, but any early sympathies were soon rejected in his teenage years, as Lewis came to see the Christian message as irrelevant and outdated, impossible to reconcile with the insights of a scientific age. For many years, as an academic in Oxford, he was to appear a staunch agnostic, yet beneath his outward scepticism he was clearly less certain, for suddenly, in the summer of 1929, he realised he could no longer deny a belief in God. That night – as he was to describe later in his book *Surprised by Joy* – he knelt down in his university rooms and prayed, committing his life to Christ. It wasn't that all his questions were answered – far from it: he was to continue wrestling with them for years to come, not least after his marriage, late in life, was cruelly cut short by the premature death of his wife from cancer. Indeed, it is probably no exaggeration to say that faith and doubt were to be his companions to the end of his life. Yet this man who had once openly scoffed at the Christian message was to become one of its greatest apologists, his *Chronicles of Narnia*, not to mention *The Screwtape Letters* and *A Grief Observed*, capturing the hearts of millions and sustaining their faith in turn.

Another equally fascinating story is that of Malcolm Muggeridge, one-time editor of *Punch* magazine and a celebrated agnostic. Dismissing Christianity for much of his life as 'a load of rubbish' and 'a religion I cannot believe', he was later to change completely, declaring: 'there must have been a resurrection because [he] is alive now, two thousand years later. There is no question at all about that.' His conversion was not a dramatic affair comparable to Paul's experience on the Damascus Road, but rather a slow evolution towards faith, or, as Muggeridge himself saw it, an unfolding spiritual journey. In 1982, Malcolm, together with his wife Kitty, joined the Catholic Church – a step which, he said, brought 'a sense of homecoming, of picking up the threads of a lost life, of responding to a bell that had long been ringing, of taking a place at a table that had long been vacant'.

Discussion points

- Do you know of others who have moved from hostility to Christ to conversion and commitment?

- It's sometimes said that converts from one cause or religion to another are more passionate about their new-found faith than those brought up in it. Do you think that's true? If so, why do you think this might be?

- Whose faith has made the most impression on you personally? What was it about them that spoke most powerfully to you?

Food for thought

Consider the following proverbs and quotations. What are they saying? Which do you find most helpful? What are their strengths and weaknesses? Do you agree or disagree with the point they're making?

- God is not an idea, or a definition that we have committed to memory; he is a presence which we experience in our hearts. (Louis Evely)

- I do not want merely to posses a faith; I want a faith that possesses me. (Charles Kingsley)

- A comprehended God is no God. (St John Chrysostom)

- To believe with certainty we must begin with doubting. (Polish proverb)

- Faith keeps many doubts in her pay. If I could not doubt, I should not believe. (Henry David Thoreau)

- Never doubt in the dark what God told you in the light. (V. Raymond Edman)

- Doubts charm me no less than knowledge. (Dante)

- Faith which does not doubt is dead faith. (Miguel de Unamuno)

- Ultimately, faith is the only key to the universe. The final meaning of human existence, and the answers to the questions on which all our happiness depends, cannot be found in any other way. (Thomas Merton)

- There lives more faith in honest doubt, believe me, than in half the creeds. (Alfred Lord Tennyson)

- Who knows nothing, doubts nothing. (French proverb)

- There are two ways to slide easily through life: to believe everything or to doubt everything; both ways save us from thinking. (Alfred Korzybski)

71

- Faith declares what the senses do not see, but not contrary to what they see. It is above them, not contrary to them. (Pascal)

- Time trieth truth in every doubt. (John Heywood)

- The wise are prone to doubt. (Greek proverb)

- I am wanting in faith . . . because I keep my eyes too much on myself, and not enough on God; I look too much on my unworthiness instead of fixing them on his goodness, his love, his sacred heart open to receive me. (Charles de Foucauld)

- It is by believing in roses that one brings them to bloom. (French proverb)

- The person who says, Unless I feel, I will not believe, is as narrow and foolish as the person who says, Unless I understand, I will not believe. (R. H. Benson)

- Deep doubts, deep wisdom; little doubts, little wisdom. (Chinese proverb)

- A faith that cannot stand collision with the truth is not worth many regrets. (Arthur C. Clarke)

- Doubt is a pain too lonely to know that faith is his twin brother. (Kahlil Gibran)

- Doubt comes in at the window when enquiry is denied at the door. (Benjamin Jowett)

Prayer

Lord, we have faith –
    enough to believe in you,
    enough to call ourselves Christians,
    but not as much as we would like,

not enough to shape every moment of life
and to touch who and what we are.
We believe, Lord:
help our unbelief.

We profess commitment and talk of all that you can do,
your ability to change lives,
your constant mercy and unfailing love,
but though we assent to such things with our minds,
they rarely touch our hearts,
filling us with the joy and peace you so long to give.
We believe, Lord:
help our unbelief.

We talk of faith that moves mountains,
that expects and attempts great things,
that is able to make a difference not just to our lives
but to the world itself,
but the faith we actually show is smaller than a mustard seed,
barely worth the name.
We believe, Lord:
help our unbelief.

Draw close to us once more,
and fill our lives with your presence.
Speak your word of life,
and reveal afresh your gracious purpose.
Capture our imagination through the love of Christ
and the transforming work of your Spirit,
so that we may have true and living faith,
nourished each day by you.
We believe, Lord:
help our unbelief.
Amen.

Completing the picture

Below are some biblical verses on the theme of faith. Reflect on them quietly together, and then discuss any further thoughts arising from them.

- Jesus did many other signs before his disciples not recorded here, but these are written so that you might believe Jesus is the Christ, the Son of God, and that, through believing, you might have life in his name. (John 20:30, 31)

- Through Jesus Christ I thank God for all of you, because your faith is being spoken of throughout the world. (Romans 1:8)

- Let us honour the name of God, for he is able to reinforce you in faith through the good news I proclaim concerning Jesus Christ – for years a hidden and secret truth but now revealed to you. (Romans 16:25)

- Your faith is not dependent on human wisdom but rests solely on God's power. (1 Corinthians 2:5)

- I want to remind you, friends, of the good news I proclaimed to you; news that you received and on which your faith remains sure. (1 Corinthians 15:1)

- We walk by faith, not by sight. (2 Corinthians 5:7)

- Above all else, grasp the shield of faith, which is able to defend you against the flaming arrows of the evil one. (Ephesians 6:16)

- So then, since we have a great high priest who has gone through the heavens, namely Jesus Christ, the Son of God, let us hold firmly to the faith we profess. (Hebrews 4:14)

- Faith is the guarantee of things hoped for, the proof of things not seen. (Hebrews 11:1)

- Keep yourselves in the love of God, my friends, building yourselves up on your most holy faith, praying in the Holy Spirit and looking forward to that day when, in his mercy, our Lord Jesus Christ will give us eternal life. (Jude vv. 20, 21)

A final word

If you were put on trial today for being a Christian, would there be enough evidence to convict you? (Anon)

Blessing

May God our Father, and our Lord Jesus Christ,
   grant peace, love and faith to all his people,
   and grace to all those with an enduring love of Christ.
Amen.

Ephesians 6:23, 24

Appendix
Answers to activities

Session 1

The eleven differences are as follows:

Pattern on flag
Time on clock
Shape of side door
Bars on lean-to window
Horizontal bar on nave window
Position and shape of cloud
Number of birds
Door handles on main door
Door handle on lean-to door
Person's arms
Roof tiles

Session 2

Odd ones out are highlighted in bold on the next page, with explanations, should you need them, given after the table.

A	Ounce	2
E	**Gramme**	4
T	Pound	**7**
U	Stone	8

Rose	**Lion**	March
Snowdrop	Cow	July
Daffodil	Sheep	May
Crocus	Horse	**June**

London	Liverpool	Silk
Bristol	Manchester Utd	Cotton
York	Tottenham Hotspur	**Nylon**
Cheltenham	**Southend Utd**	Wool

Hebrews	Holland	**Rain**
Exodus	France	Snow
Romans	Belgium	Frost
Acts	**Brazil**	Ice

Level	Football	Nahum
Wide	**Golf**	Nehemiah
Deed	Rugby	**Ruth**
Tenet	Hockey	Timothy

- T is not a vowel
- A gramme is a metric weight; the rest are imperial
- 7 is an odd number

- The rose is a summer-flowering shrub; the rest are spring-flowering bulbs
- The lion is carnivorous; the other animals here are herbivores
- June has 30 days; the others have 31
- Cheltenham, unlike London, Bristol and York, is not a city
- Liverpool, Manchester United and Spurs are all Premier League sides; Southend United, sadly, are not . . . or at least not yet!
- Nylon is a synthetic material; the rest are all made from natural materials
- Exodus is an Old Testament book; the rest are from the New Testament
- Brazil is in South America; the other countries are all in Europe
- Snow, frost and ice are all frozen, unlike rain
- 'Level', 'deed' and 'tenet' read the same whichever way you read them, unlike 'wide'
- Golf is usually an individual game; the others are always team games
- Nahum, Nehemiah and Timothy are books of the Bible named after men; Ruth is a book of the Bible named after a woman

Session 3

The letters can be rearranged to spell out:

I AM THE RESURRECTION AND THE LIFE

Session 4

The stages I've used to get from one word to the other are as follows:

POOR	SELF	TAKE	HURT	GREED
POOL	SELL	TAME	CURT	BREED
POLL	CELL	GAME	CULT	BLEED
POLE	CULL	GAVE	CULL	BLEND
PILE	CURL	GIVE	HULL	BLAND
RILE	CURE		HELL	BLANK
RICE	CARE		HEAL	CLANK
RICH				CLINK
				CHINK
				THINK
				THANK
				SHANK
				SPANK
				SPARK
				SPARE
				SCARE
				SHARE

There are, of course, other ways of getting from A to B.

Session 5

There is no difference in any of the lines, dots or circles – they're exactly the same in each case!